Verses by Christian Morgenstern
Translated by Helga Barthold
& John Theobald

A Star & Elephant Book
from
The Green Tiger Press
La Jolla, California 92038
Copyright© 1980

Originally published by Bruno Cassirer
Berlin, 1920

ISBN 0-914676-38-5

Color Separation by
Color Graphics, San Diego, California

Type set in Tiffany Demi-bold by
Thompson Type, San Diego, California

Printing by
Publishers Press, Salt Lake City, Utah

The
Rabbit Book
of
k. F. E. von Freyhold
÷
A Star & Elephant Book

I am the Easter prince, soon to be king.
My trumpet and pretzel say, "Here comes the Spring!"

At night, while Paul sleeps dreaming on the lawn,
The Easter bunnies steal up before dawn,
With one egg under his hand to slide
and one in the crook of his elbow to hide.
The moon stands up on the sky and thinks, "Drat!
I don't get a present as nice as that!"

Fritz opened the window. Amazed he stared
At the Easter splendor all over the yard:
On all the flower beds and along the wall,
See! hundreds of eggs! O look at them all!

Low in the sky is the rising sun.
The Easter bunny starts his run.
There's a basket of eggs and over it peers
A group of three rabbits who prick up their ears.

The Easter bunny is laying an egg.
A butterfly almost alights on his leg.
The sea is shining far away,
And beside it a sandy beach to play.

The Easter eggs were scarcely laid down
When Kurt popped up there looking for one.

Our baby girl finds a heap of them there,
With a white and a blue one just waiting for her.

There's an egg for every blossom's cup.
See! everywhere now they are showing up!

Little Paul, getting tired beneath the bright sun,
Falls asleep in the field before morning is done.
The bells are ringing: bim, bam, beam.
While Paul smiles tenderly in his dream.

Diddle diddle dum, diddle diddle do,
We dance with our bunny,
Clasping closely two by two
On the grass where it's sunny.

Diddle diddle dum, diddle diddle do,
We dance on the lawn,
Left and right are sitting two
That toot on their horn.

Diddle diddle dum, diddle diddle do,
We dance with our bunny,
Clasping closely two by two
On the grass where it's sunny.

One of the bunnies says to another,
"Let's go inside for a look, little brother!"

Can you imagine Baby-girl's face
When she sees bunnies sitting around the place?

With bells and violins the dance
Of these musical bunnies will now commence.

One pipes, three are rocked to sleep in the arms
Of the children wanting to keep them from harm.

The chocolate is ready for Easter's sake,
And now it is time to have some cake.

Now all of us kiss and gather some flowers
And so to an end with this Easter of ours.